CORNW

THE HIDDEN LAND

by

RICHARD & ANN JENKIN

with

A new Introduction by

PROFESSOR PHILIP PAYTON

and a new timeline 1965-2005 by

Ann Trevenen Jenkin.

Second edition re-published by Noonvares Press 2005.

CORNWALL
LIBRARY

Cornwall the Hidden Land

First published in 1965 by West Country Publications.

Second facsimile edition published with additions by Noonvares Press, An Gernyk, Leedstown, Hayle TR27 6BA, Cornwall, UK. Tel:01736-850332. Email: trevenen@tesco.net. November 2005.

Printed by Troutbeck Press, Mabe, Penryn, Kernow.

Tel: 01326-373226.

ISBN 0 9524601 5 7

Preface 2005

This little booklet is republished 40 years after the original production in 1965.

It is re-issued with a new introduction by Professor Philip Payton, Director of the Institute of Cornish Studies at the University of Exeter in Cornwall at Tremough, Penryn. This is appropriate as the authors, forty years ago, were already pressing for a Cornish University. Thanks to him for his generous comments.

There is an additional postscript by myself as the surviving author, with a timeline of important developments affecting the life and identity of Cornwall since 1965, with some implicit comments on how the Cornish World has changed for better or worse. Any errors, omissions or opinions are my own. Otherwise, the book is a facsimile reproduction of the original.

This second edition is dedicated to the memory of **Richard Jenkin (1925-2002)** the co-author, who in the last forty years had done more than most people to see that his dreams of a future Cornwall were realised. He led or was involved with most Cornish initiatives, linguistic, political and cultural. He died in October 2002, but had already heard about the Cornish Language being recognised on the Charter for Minority European languages. He was delighted.

May this timely reprint of *Cornwall the Hidden Land* remind us of how much has been achieved for Kernow and the Cornish people but how much more remains to be done.

Kernow bys Vyken.

Ann Trevenen Jenkin

Leedstown. October 2005.

Acknowledgements

Agreement has been given by Mebyon Kernow, the publishers of the Cornish Calendar, for the re-use of illustrations from the original booklet. Where possible individual authors have also been contacted. Some had died or could not be traced. Thanks to all who have supported this re-print, including Pol Hodge, Dr. Garry Tregidga, Dick Cole, Donald Rawe and other friends for help with the timeline. Thanks especially to Dick Gendall for the cover design.

Thanks to Joy Menhennet for the use of the photograph.

Corrections of Errors still in the original facsimile text

p. 14. Rudolph Raspe

P. 21 line 6. ..'of his sitters'

P. 22 Nicky Nan Reservist.

P. 24 …la boule

P. 25 Bishop Trelawny.

P. 27 line 2 omission of 'of'.

INTRODUCTION

Some forty-five years ago, I acquired my copy of *Cornwall the Hidden Land* by Richard and Ann Jenkin; a modest slim, pea-green pamphlet whose impact upon me was to be profound.

As an ardent Cornish enthusiast, full of schoolboy energy and inquisitiveness, I devoted a great deal of time in my later teenage years to searching out Cornish material – browsing in libraries, scouring second-hand bookshops, sending off for publishers' lists. Amongst the latter, was the catalogue of a small publishing house in Bracknell (of all places!), whose unpromisingly titled series *West Country Handbooks,* concealed the altogether more enticing title *Cornwall the Hidden Land* – which at a pocket money price I could afford, (4s6d!) seemed to me a 'must'.

The postal order was despatched, and by return came the little volume that was to prove so important. For Richard and Ann Jenkin had provided what was in effect a manifesto for modern Cornwall. It was a manifesto rooted in the Revivalist tradition of 'Celtic Cornwall' but which attempted to reconcile Cornwall's ancient Celticity – not least the Cornish language itself – with the culture of industrial Cornwall: the world of Richard Trevithick, Billy Bray, engine houses, brass bands, and global emigration. It was a powerful synthesis, a heady mix, and what's more it was persuasive – for me at least.

And there was a strong political edge that also appealed. Describing the foundation of Mebyon Kernow in 1951, the authors insisted: *The emergence over the last fifteen years or so of a thoughtful, vocal and consciously Cornish group is one of the most promising signs that Cornwall will continue to exist as a Celtic Country and not decline into merely an administrative division of England.* Indeed it was.

Calling for *a form of self-government within Great Britain,* Richard and Ann Jenkin advocated a Cornish Assembly long before devolution was the order of the day in the United Kingdom, anticipating the activities of the Cornish Constitutional Convention which in the early twenty-first century organised a petition of 50,000 signatures echoing their demand. They also called for a Cornish University: *Mebyon Kernow advocates the establishment of a University in Cornwall and greater emphasis on Cornwall and its culture.* Although the new Combined Universities in Cornwall Campus at Tremough is not yet the fully-fledged Cornish University the authors had in mind, it is evidence of significant institutional renewal in Cornwall, and is a base from which a more overtly Cornish agenda might emerge. Likewise, although the Cornish economy remains dangerously over-reliant on tourism, there is now recognition that Cornwall must develop a more sustainable future, an echo of the view advanced by Richard and Ann Jenkin – *Mebyon Kernow believes that Cornwall needs a stable and broad-based economy and a developing cultural life.*

Over forty years after its publication, *Cornwall the Hidden Land* remains a lively and relevant contribution to understanding the past, present and future of Cornwall. Its reappearance now is timely and will be welcomed by Cornish people the world over.

Professor Philip Payton, Director, Institute of Cornish Studies,

University of Exeter in Cornwall.

CORNWALL
the hidden land

RICHARD & ANN JENKIN

West Country Handbook No. 2.   4s 6d

CORNWALL : THE HIDDEN LAND

by RICHARD & ANN JENKIN

EDITORS of NEW CORNWALL

The realised image of Cornwall is filled with healing

Renée Haynes

THE CROSSING AT MALPAS
from "Trystan hag Ysolt" by Caradar

Grateful acknowledgement is made to Mebyon Kernow, publishers of the yearly Cornish Calendar, and to the artists for permission to reproduce these illustrations.

CORNWALL—THE HIDDEN LAND

by RICHARD & ANN JENKIN

Most visitors to Cornwall receive a distinct impression of difference. One holiday-maker said "Here we get the feel of a foreign holiday without the language difficulty". This impression is the result of many subtle, even sub-conscious, observations. The more discerning visitor feels it most strongly.

This little book is intended to indicate to both the interested visitor and the enquiring Cornishman some of the realities that lie beneath the obvious surface differences between Cornwall and the lands across the Tamar. It does not set out to be a guide book, nor is it a complete survey of Cornish history or Cornish culture.

CORNWALL AND ITS LANGUAGE

One of the most immediate impressions of Cornwall's "difference" is given by the un-English place-names which greet the visitor as soon as he arrives in Cornwall: — from Kelly Bray to Penzance, from Lesnewth to Landewednack, Trewardreva, Polgooth and Penstrassow. These are echoed in many Cornish surnames which are derived from place-names: — Trembath, Polglaze, Pentreath, Roscorla, Lanyon. Welsh visitors will notice immediately a similarity to Welsh place-names, disguised though it may be by spelling.

The explanation is that for most of their long history the Cornish spoke their own language which continued in daily use by a diminishing number of people until just over 150 years ago. Since that time English has been the daily language of Cornwall, though knowledge of Cornish, both scholarly and traditional, has never

3

completely died out. Scraps of Cornish have been passed down orally in family traditions and there have always been some scholars with a fair knowledge of the language. The place-names and family names are living Cornish in the mouths of the people, even if they do not always know their meaning.

The Cornish language is very like Welsh. It is even more like Breton, which is the modern form of the language carried to that part of the Continent by emigrants from Cornwall and South Britain in the 5th and 6th Centuries A.D. Welsh, Cornish and Breton belong to the Celtic group of languages which also includes Irish, Manx and Scots Gaelic.

Popular interest in Cornish began to revive about 80 years ago, and the efforts of the pioneers resulted in the formation in 1920 of the Federation of Old Cornwall Societies, which links together the thousands of Cornish people who are interested in the language, history and culture of their own land. There are now 37 Old Cornwall Societies in the Federation, from Penzance to Saltash, from St. Just-in-Penwith to Bude and Stratton.

Even earlier, in 1904, the pioneers of the cultural revival gained acceptance of Cornwall as a full member of the Second Pan-Celtic Congress in Caernarvon, and Cornwall has continued to be represented at the Celtic Congresses. The Congress meets once a year in one of the Celtic countries to discuss cultural and social matters and to co-ordinate efforts to maintain the Celtic traditions of these countries. Since the war Cornwall has taken its turn in acting as host to the Celtic Congress in 1950, 1956, and 1963.

In 1928 the revival of interest in the Cornish language and culture had progressed so far that it was possible to realize one of the aims of the pioneers by establishing a Gorsedd of Bards for Cornwall, similar to the Breton Gorsedd (founded 1901) and the Welsh Gorsedd, whose ceremonies are familiar to all who have seen the Welsh Royal National Eisteddfod.

On the first Saturday in September you may see the procession of blue-robed Cornish Bards making its way to a chosen site where it performs in Cornish an impressive ceremony symbolising the

4

TRISTAN'S LEAP

Mary Mills

loyalty of the Cornish to their land, their language and their Celtic culture. The Bards are supported by members of the Old Cornwall Societies, with their Society Banners, and often there are delegates from the Welsh and Breton Gorsedds, bringing fraternal greetings. The next day there is a service in Cornish in a local church.

The Cornish Gorsedd differs from the other two in that all its members are Bards and there are no Druids or Ovates. A Cornish Bard can be distinguished from a Welsh or Breton Bard by the black and gold bars on his head-dress. Who are these Bards? Entry into the Gorsedd is limited to those who are judged worthy for work they have done in the arts, music, literature, historical or archaeological research for their knowledge of Cornish; or for great services to Cornwall and Cornish culture.

Each year the Gorsedd organises essay competitions for school-children, public competitions in musical composition, and in verse and prose in Cornish and English, the first prizes being presented at the Gorsedd Ceremony. As so many people are now learning Cornish the Gorsedd sets examinations in three grades— Elementary, Intermediate and Advanced, the Advanced standard being equivalent to G.C.E. in a foreign language, and the Examinations Board acts as guardian of the linguistic standards of Cornish.

Cornish, though not the easiest language to learn, is musical and very expressive and has attracted many writers. A number of books in modern Cornish have been published (see Bibliography page 28), and many more would be if costs were less. In addition, Cornish is used on items such as Calendars, Christmas Cards, and souvenirs, which have proved very popular. Cornish people very frequently choose names in Cornish for their houses and there is much more knowledge about Cornish than there was half a century ago.

CORNWALL'S MAY FESTIVALS

Spring and early Summer in Cornwall is a magic season with a clear freshness more exhilarating than the crowded and dusty late summer. Those who are fortunate enough to be in Cornwall at the beginning of May should make every effort to visit Padstow

5

on May Day and Helston on Furry Day.

It is a stirring and shaking experience to be in Padstow as the 'Obby 'Oss makes his round, performing his ritual death and regeneration in every street. The rhythmic drum-beat and varying tempo of the singing arouse emotions that stem from the earliest ages of man. But it has to be experienced to be appreciated.

A week later, on May 8th (or on the previous Saturday if the 8th is a Sunday or a Monday) the infectious lilt of the Furry Dance fills the Helston air. Heralded by the rumbustious Hal an Tow ceremony, the day brings its own blend of dignity and gaiety as later the dancers take their traditional route around the town, through the streets and through the houses.

Though incidental parts of these ceremonies can be dated to the Medieval and even later periods, the tradition is a long one, stretching back to nature rites of older religions, christianised in succeeding ages. The purpose of both is to welcome summer—in the Helston Hal an Tow song we sing "For summer is a come-o and winter is a gone-o", and in Padstow "Adieu the merry spring— for summer is a-come unto day". The 1st of May (Cala' Me in Cornish) is the first day of summer in the old Celtic year, as November 1st (Calan Gwaf) is the first day of Winter. These were the two great festivals of the year, celebrated by dancing and bonfires, the first, Beltaine, the day of reviving life, the second, Samain, the day of the dead, (All Hallows). As fires played a large part in these ceremonies, is it merely co-incidence that the November 5th Guy Fawkes fires rapidly achieved a popularity which has far outlasted their political significance?

Other important dates in the Celtic year were Midsummer Eve, which, in Cornwall, is still celebrated with bonfires, and the winter solstice, the rites of which have been absorbed in Christmas Day.

The long continued observance of these celebrations, modified as they have been from time to time, is a testimony to the strength and endurance of tradition in Cornwall.

6

OLD CROSS AT MAWGAN IN PYDAR
The late K. O. Chetwood-Aiken

CORNWALL'S ANCIENT STONES

Cornwall has a wealth of ancient stone memorials—crosses, menhirs, dolmens, ston e-circles—to be found both in remote moors and by busy modern roads. They are not all equally old, the stone circles, dolmens, and simple menhirs dating from the Neolithic and Bronze ages, while the crosses of various types date from earliest Christian times to the Medieval period after the English conquest.

Not all the menhirs or standing stones are pre-Christian. The tradition of marking the graves of great men with standing stones continued up to the English conquest and many of these memorials have the name of the dead leader inscribed on them. Far away in the west, in a remote valley between two rough hil's, stands the Men Scryfa (Stone of Writing). On this stone can easily be seen the inscription:— RIALOBRANI CUNOVALI FILI—(the stone of) Rialobran son of Cunoval, names that echo those of Caratacus son of Cunobelinus, and Cassivellaunus, who confronted the Romans, and which testify to the continued existence of the royal Celtic families after the Roman departure.

In the east of Cornwall, near St. Cleer, another memorial, which probably formed the shaft of a finely decorated Celtic cross, is inscribed DONIERT ROGAVIT PRO ANIMA—Doniert asks (prayers) for (his) soul—, a memorial to a Cornish king who lived about the time of the English King Alfred. These scores of memorial stones—and there were probably many more that have not survived the ravages of time and man—are the relics of a political Cornwall, unsubdued by the English, which endured from the time of the Romans and the arrival of the English to within a century or so of the conquest of the English themselves by the Normans.

The most romantic of these memorials stands at a cross-roads near Fowey, not far from its original site. Its inscription has been read as DRUSTANUS IC IACIT CUNOMORI FILIUS. The early manuscript Life of St. Pol de Leon tells us that King Mark of Cornwall was named Marcus Quono-morus. If the reading of the inscription is correct, this stone may be the actual memorial of Trystan, son (not nephew) of Mark, and the beloved of Ysolt of Ireland. Professor Loth, in his examination of the earliest available forms of the Trystan story, was able

7

to identify the setting and place-names with the south coast districts of Cornwall. Here the ill-starred lovers played out their tragedy. In the earliest versions Mark's palace was never at Tintagel but at Lancien—now Lantyan, a farm near the earthwork of Castle Dor. Excavations there by Mr. Ralegh Radford F.S.A. have shown that this Iron Age fort was re-used in the post-Roman period, so this was probably Mark's fortress, and we may claim a historical basis for the story of Trystan of Cornwall. It has been said that Trystan or Drustan is a pictish name and therefore the story must have originated in Scotland, but names do travel,—Geoffrey Chaucer cannot be claimed for France merely because Geoffrey is a French name, nor are all the modern Donalds and Grahams of Scots descent.

Little, unfortunately, is known about the Kings in Cornwall, and at times there seem to have been several sub-kings, united only in opposition to the English. The final absorption of Cornwall by England may have occurred through the failure of the Royal Cornish line and a subsequent power-vacuum rather than a direct conquest. A great deal of confusion has been caused by the failure of the old chroniclers to distinguish clearly between the Kingdom of Cornwall (Kernow) and the old Kingdom of Cornouaille (Kernev) in Brittany.

THE SAINTS OF CORNWALL AND EARLY RELIGIOUS LIFE

Apart from the wealth of Cornish place-names and family names one other difference which the visitor will notice is the astonishing variety of Saints' names used in church dedications and village names. He will be able to visit St. Piran's Oratory, an early church, for long lost in the sands at Perranzabuloe. He can go to St. Mabyn, St. Kew, St. Endellion, St. Ruan Lanihorne, St. Issey, St. Clether, St. Levan, St. Erth and many others. The inherent music of the names makes one wonder where these saints came from and why their names are so different from the dedications of most English churches.

Christianity was brought to Cornwall by the Romans, but it did not become a coherent and vital force in the lives of the Cornish until the Age of the Saints in the 5th and 6th Centuries. Then,

8

to identify the setting and place-names with the south coast districts of Cornwall. Here the ill-starred lovers played out their tragedy. In the earliest versions Mark's palace was never at Tintagel but at Lancien—now Lantyan, a farm near the earthwork of Castle Dor. Excavations there by Mr. Ralegh Radford F.S.A. have shown that this Iron Age fort was re-used in the post-Roman period, so this was probably Mark's fortress, and we may claim a historical basis for the story of Trystan of Cornwall. It has been said that Trystan or Drustan is a pictish name and therefore the story must have originated in Scotland, but names do travel,—Geoffrey Chaucer cannot be claimed for France merely because Geoffrey is a French name, nor are all the modern Donalds and Grahams of Scots descent.

Little, unfortunately, is known about the Kings in Cornwall, and at times there seem to have been several sub-kings, united only in opposition to the English. The final absorption of Cornwall by England may have occurred through the failure of the Royal Cornish line and a subsequent power-vacuum rather than a direct conquest. A great deal of confusion has been caused by the failure of the old chroniclers to distinguish clearly between the Kingdom of Cornwall (Kernow) and the old Kingdom of Cornouaille (Kernev) in Brittany.

THE SAINTS OF CORNWALL AND EARLY RELIGIOUS LIFE

Apart from the wealth of Cornish place-names and family names one other difference which the visitor will notice is the astonishing variety of Saints' names used in church dedications and village names. He will be able to visit St. Piran's Oratory, an early church, for long lost in the sands at Perranzabuloe. He can go to St. Mabyn, St. Kew, St. Endellion, St. Ruan Lanihorne, St. Issey, St. Clether, St. Levan, St. Erth and many others. The inherent music of the names makes one wonder where these saints came from and why their names are so different from the dedications of most English churches.

Christianity was brought to Cornwall by the Romans, but it did not become a coherent and vital force in the lives of the Cornish until the Age of the Saints in the 5th and 6th Centuries. Then,

8

MENACUDDLE WELL

Alice Butler

successive bands of Saints and their followers came to Cornwall either to settle or to travel on in their journeyings between Wales, Ireland, Brittany and other parts of Europe. Visitors from other Celtic countries will be familiar with many of the Celtic Saints' names which are found in Cornwall: —St. Sampson in Brittany and Wales, St. Petroc (Pedrog) in Wales, St. Fimbarrus (Fionbarr) in Ireland, St. Gwinear (Fingar) in Ireland and Wales, and many others. Cornwall had its own saints too, St. Constantine, who was a king of Cornwall, and St. Cuby who went to Wales and founded a monastery at Holyhead (Pen Caer Cybi).

Not much is known about many of these saints though you will find legends about their lives everywhere. Some of these legends are based on fact, and stories of saints suffering tortures and hardships and mortifying their earthly desires were certainly pictorial representations of the difficulties and dangers of their lives. Sixth century Cornwall was lonely and isolated, compared with many other parts of Britain and many of the early saints deliberately chose the wildest places they could, in order to find peace and opportunity for contemplation. The Saints' Holy Wells, and often the churches too, are in out-of-the-way spots far from the present centres of population. This is true up to medieval times. Visit St. Melor's Well at Linkinhorne, the largest Holy Well in Cornwall at St. Clether or the delightfully situated Holy Well at Menacuddle and see how isolated they seem, even today. Because of this, however, they still suggest the atmosphere of loneliness and dogged determination which characterised these men and women of so long ago.

Lives of many of the Cornish Saints were studied in a most able fashion by the late Canon Doble (see Bibliography) but apart from his books there is a Cornish play "Bewnans Meryasek" (The Life of St. Meriasek or Meriadoc) which gives some interesting information about the life of one Cornish saint. This play is unique, though it is probable that there were other plays about Cornish saints which have been lost. The play itself is wholly in the Cornish language. It was copied by a cleric, Ralph or Richard Ton in 1504, possibly from an older Glasney original, and tells the story of St. Meriasek, who was born in Brittany, but who spent much of his missionary life at Camborne in Cornwall until he was forced to

9

flee because the pagan King Teudar threatened to kill him. The rest of the play, apart from interpolated legends about St. Silvester and Emperor Constantine and the Virgin's Rescue of a widow's son, deals with the later life of Meriasek in Brittany.

There are other Cornish plays too, mostly on religious themes, and with 'The Life of St. Meriasek' they form the bulk of our early literature. The most well known to students of literature is the late fourteenth century play-cycle known by its latin title of the 'Ordinalia' which was written in three sections:—The Origin of the World; The Passion of Christ; The Resurrection of The Lord. These were performed out of doors on three successive days. These 'Miracle Plays', as they were called, did much to keep Cornish alive, for it is known from the plans in the texts and from the stage directions that the performance of the plays was the occasion for much festivity. Plays were performed in 'Rounds' or 'Playing Places' (Cornish:— Plen an gwary) up and down the countryside. The most famous Round still existing is Perran Round near Perranzabuloe, but the Plen an Gwary at St. Just-in-Penwith is easier to find as it is right in the middle of the town. Standing in the centre of one of these Rounds it is possible to imagine the scene—the whole story of God's dealings with Mankind from the Creation of The World to The Ascension of Christ. These plays were not dull religious sermonizings either, for there is much rumbustious humour like that in the English Miracle Play Cycles, further enlivened by local references which must have gone down well with the audience. The cast must have been tremendous and their energy indefatigable to keep acting for three days. As most of the actors were local and known to the audience the participation of the spectators in the events portrayed was always subjective. The scenes became a part of the small community where they were actea. This sympathetic response between actor and spectator is lost in our more sophisticated world.

CORNWALL AND NONCOMFORMITY

If, one Whit Monday, you are wandering near Redruth you may be surprised to hear hymn singing apparently rising out of the ground. Closer investigation will disclose several thousand people in a large sunken amphitheatre. This is the famous Gwennap Pit, a place of pilgrimage for Methodists who each year celebrate the

10

- 21 -

BILLY BRAY

Richard Gendall

evangelical work of John Wesley in Cornwall.

Wesley made many journeys in Cornwall and his work produced a profound change. On his first journeys he was hounded by magistrates and mobs on the absurd suspicion that he was a Jacobite agent. His followers were persecuted and press-ganged. But his earnestness and religious fervour struck echoes in the emotional souls of the Cornish people and his last journeys were almost triumphal tours. Though many of the gentry still feared his "religious enthusiasm" many of his critics were forced to admit the improvement in sobriety and honesty that the Methodist movement had brought about. The main social evils in Cornwall then were the violence engendered by harsh underpaid work in the mines, and the disregard of laws and widespread drunkenness arising from the wholesale addiction to smuggling. Though some, like Harry Carter, of Prussia Cove, were able to combine Methodism with a firm belief in the justice of "The Free Trade", Wesley himself set his face steadfastly against smuggling, drunkenness and violence.

The Cornish at the Reformation had found the Anglican services so little to their religious taste that they had risen in armed revolt. Their love for their ancient parish churches, hallowed by the worship of their forefathers, might have eventually reconciled them to the New Order, but, with some honourable exceptions, the clergy of the Augustan Age were out of touch with the spiritual needs of their flocks and religious life sank into apathy. The Methodist movement, with its emphasis on lay-participation, gave scope to the Cornish need for religious experience that was unsatisfied by the modest and unemotional Anglican services. There was more in common between a Methodist Revival meeting and a Pre-Reformation Corpus Christi Procession or a Miracle Play than would appear on the surface. Restricted by set services and starved of outlets for religious feeling, the Cornish gave themselves whole-heartedly to Methodism. Chapels and Meeting-houses sprang up everywhere. Bible reading raised the general standards of education, and lay preaching provided opportunities for public speaking,—the practical experience so gained was later carried over into political and social causes. Altogether the strict moral standards of Methodism raised the whole moral tone of Cornwall.

11

- 23 -

One celebrated "local preacher" was Billy Bray, a miner from Twelveheads. He is still remembered for his sincere Christian life, his great activity as a chapel builder, and the homely wit and vivid turn of phrase of his sermons. It was Billy who said, "I don't believe our Father meant for men to smoke. If he did, He'd have put a hole in the top of their heads; for 'tisn't no heavenly architect that'd leave the smoke to go out the front door."

After Wesley's death secessionist groups arose and were all fully represented in Cornwall. Cornwall itself contributed one group, the Bible Christians or Bryanites, and the chapels multiplied, two or three in every village and half a dozen in each of the towns. These sometimes gaunt, sometimes primitively sturdy, buildings remain as mute witnesses to the amazing religious ferment, though the subsequent reunion of various Methodist groups rendered many of them redundant, some to be turned into workshops, warehouses or dwellings. At one time Methodism was practically the established church of Cornwall and today the majority in Cornwall are still nominally Methodists, though with the lessening of differences between church and chapel the church has regained some lost ground.

The Methodist Revival was not all gain, however. The new sobriety led many of the stricter members to frown on all more or less innocent fun. Cornish people are enthusiastic singers and sing naturally in harmony. This love of singing and the composing of carols was maintained and developed by the chapel choirs, but disapproval of secular songs began to kill off folk songs and dances, and many must have been lost. Art, drama and literature, except for moral tales, were under similar condemnation and the "idle stories"—folk-tales or drolls—passed from the memory of the people, though fortunately some of them were recorded in time and printed, notably by Hunt and Bottrell.

CORNWALL'S MINING

As one travels the length and breadth of Cornwall one sees,— dominating the skyline, sheltering in secluded valleys, lonely in the midst of moors, down the back-streets of the inland towns, even clinging to cliffs,—the ubiquitous Cornish engine houses. Their

12

CHARGING A ROUND IN A DRIFT

Mary Mills

sturdy four-square, three-storey granite towers, each with a tall chimney like an admonitory finger pointing a moral, have been likened by imaginative visitors to ruined Norman keeps.

To the Cornishman these ruined relics of past industry have a significance greater than that of any Norman castle. These are the memorials of a way of life—now practically disappeared—which was rooted in the distant past yet formed modern Cornwall. Mining rose through the centuries to be the dominant economic factor in Cornwall and then in a comparatively short time was practically wiped out. The resulting economic upheaval affected the vast majority of families in Cornwall and resulted in a drastic re-arrangement of population. Its psychological effects can still be traced today.

Cornish mines have produced mainly tin and copper, though lead, arsenic and wolfram have also been worked. Tin was extracted in Cornwall in the Bronze Ages from alluvial deposits, and in the Iron Age, was exported to Ireland, Western Europe and the Mediterranean, though there is little or no evidence for extraction in Post-Roman times until the early Middle Ages. This may be because the evidence has been destroyed by later workings. The working of alluvial deposits became important again in the 12th and 13th centuries, though at first the workings around Dartmoor were more important than those in Cornwall. Even so, all the tin workings in the West were under the general control of the Earl of Cornwall, and it was the wealth derived from them that enabled Richard, Earl of Cornwall, Count of Poitou, brother of Henry III, to buy his election as "King of the Romans" in 1257 as a first step in his unachieved ambition to become the "Holy Roman Emperor". Cornwall produced practically all Europe's tin and the economic importance of this was so great that the English kings ensured that the Earldom of Cornwall was held only by a member of the Royal Family, or occasionally by the King's current favourite. Eventually Edward I created the Duchy of Cornwall, to be held always by the eldest son of the King of England. This was the first use of the title of Duke by the English. (At that time Duchies were often semi-independent states and powerful dukes likes those of Normandy, Brittany, Burgundy, Luxemburg, etc., sometimes claimed royal prerogatives.)

13

The Cornish tinners, of course, saw little of the wealth their labour produced, but they were such an important source of economic strength that they were given special treatment. They were freed from local feudal dues and duties and were subject only to their own Stannary Courts under the authority of the Duke. No case involving a tinner could be tried except in their own courts, which was certainly a privilege! They were not liable for military service under the Lord-Lieutenant, but formed their own regiments under the Lord Warden of the Stannaries. (The difficulties inherent in this were sometimes overcome by giving both offices to one man. In Elizabeth's reign Sir Walter Raleigh held both offices for a time.) The tinners were allowed to prospect on any man's land and to divert streams required for water-power. In effect, the tinners formed a state within a state, and even in non-mining matters the Duchy Council exercised most of the prerogatives which were reserved to the King's officers in other counties.

In Tudor times the alluvial deposits were worked out and the tinners began to follow the lodes into the ground with open-cast workings and horizontal drifts into hillsides. This was the beginning of underground mining and in the next century "experts" from Germany came to superintend the new methods. One of the less reputable of these was Rudolp Raspe who wrote 'The Adventures of Baron Munchausen'. The Cornishmen learnt quickly, and drove their mines deeper and deeper, using vertical shafts. The limiting factors to the working depth were the supply of air and the presence of water. These problems were dealt with by the construction of adits and miners became very proficient in driving these gently graded tunnels often for several miles to a suitable outlet.

At the dawn of the Industrial Revolution the Cornish mining engineers were quick to take advantage of Watt's application of steam power to machinery, and used his pumping engine to enable them to mine deeper. Many improvements were made, such as Trevithick's use of high pressure steam. Watt, who believed it dangerous, declared that Trevithick ought to be hanged. Many attempts were made to circumvent Boulton and Watt's all-too-embracing patents and Watt sent Murdoch down to Redruth to represent his firm's interests. While in Redruth Murdoch invented gas-lighting and he also designed a model self-propelled steam

14

engine. Boulton and Watt dissuaded him from "wasting" his time in this way and it was left to Trevithick to produce the first passenger-carrying steam locomotive at Camborne in 1801 and in 1804 the first railway locomotive at Merthyr Tydfil, South Wales, —ten years before Stephenson's first locomotive. The development of road steam-cars was left to another Cornish engineer, Sir Goldsworthy Gurney, who invented the forced steam draught that Stephenson used on his "Rocket". But vested interests combined to drive the steam car off the roads.

In the middle of the 19th century Cornwall was producing three quarters of the world's copper and nearly half the tin; but times were getting harder with the opening of mines in America, Australia, South Africa, and later the working of alluvial tin in Malaya. The price of copper and tin started to fall and the Great Emigration began. Cornishmen—the leading experts in metalliferous mining—spread all over the world to the copper mines of the Great Lakes; the silver, mercury and gold mines of California; the copper and gold mines of Australia; and those of South Africa and South America. Wherever they went they formed close-knit communities, keeping up their home customs and building their Methodist Chapels. These Bible-reading, sober, withdrawn, and hard-working Cornishmen filled the skilled and responsible positions in the mines, until it was said that wherever there was a hole in the ground you would find a Cornishman at the bottom of it.

During the Great Emigration thousands of Cornishmen left home each year—most never to return. Hardly a family in Cornwall has not some relatives abroad and there are probably more people of Cornish descent overseas than are left in Cornwall. The older Cornishmen are often more familiar with Ballarat, San Francisco or Natal than with Bradford, Swindon or Nottingham. This mass migration, under economic pressure, of the more active part of the Cornish population has had profound psychological effects as well as the more obvious results of ruined mines and miners' cottages. There is still a bitter suspicion of the economic system that has caused, and continues to cause, the emigration (nowadays mainly to England) of many of the more talented Cornishmen. The continuing family links with America, Australia and South Africa give the Cornish a different outlook on the world from that of the

15

English, and there is a certain nostalgia for the days when Cornwall was one of the leading industrial areas of Britain.

In the last year or so there has been a revival of interest in the Cornish tin-mines as the alluvial deposits in Malaya are nearing exhaustion. In addition to the two mines, Geevor and South Crofty, that have continued working through the depressed years, schemes are afoot to re-open mines in several parts of Cornwall and also to work off-shore lodes that have not yet been tapped.

Growing out of the needs of the mines, an engineering tradition developed in Cornwall which enabled Holman Brothers and the Climax Rock Drill Co. to maintain their position as leading mining machinery manufacturers even when the Cornish home market had practically disappeared. The famous engineering firm of Tangye Bros. was founded by a Cornish family; the Healey of Austin-Healeys is a Cornishman, as was the original founder of the Belling Light Engineering Co. which became the Belling Electric Co., and Cornwall has produced many famous engineers as well as miners.

CORNWALL'S CHINA CLAY

Travelling through the south central area of Cornwall the dominant feature is the multitude of great white pyramids—the "sky-tips" of waste sand from the china clay works. While some see them as vast sterile wastes others find a strange impressive grandeur in them as changing light reveals ever-varying aspects. If you explore around the feet of these man-made hills you will find abandoned workings, almost bottomless pits of deep green water, smiling yet treacherous. Some of the clay pits now being worked are tremendous, great gashes torn our of the earth, huge craters several miles in circumference and thousands of feet deep, the buildings and machinery at the bottom dwarfed by the sheer sides of the chasm.

The secret of making true porcelain was discovered in Europe in 1709 and so the monopoly that the Chinese had held since the ninth century was brought to an end. Thomas Cookworthy, a Quaker chemist of South Devon, prospected for Kaolin (china

16

AN OLD BEAM ENGINE

Richard Gendall

clay), the essential raw material for porcelain, and first discovered it at Tregonning Hill, Breage. Later it was found in other parts of Cornwall, especially the St. Stephens—St. Dennis—St. Austell area. Cookworthy used the Cornish china clay and china-stone in his Plymouth porcelain works, which were later moved to Bristol. Cornwall provided the raw materials for the English china industry and scores of uses for china clay have since been developed. Only 10% of the production is now used for pottery. The main use now is in paper-manufacture—about 75% of the annual production of more than $1\frac{1}{2}$ million tons. It is also used in textiles, rubber, tooth-paste, face-powder, medicine, soap and paint! Some of the waste sand is used in making concrete blocks and the other by-product, mica, finds a variety of uses including the "glitter" on Christmas cards.

This vast industry started as mining entered a period of depression and the machinery and skills of the miners were adapted to the new industry. The method of extraction is to direct very high pressure water jets at the rock face. A sludge collects at the lowest part of the pit and is run into pools where the coarse quartz sand settles. The milky suspension of china clay and mica is pumped to the surface where it is passed through settling tanks where the remaining sand and mica are left behind. The pumping was formerly carried out by the same "Cornish Beam Engines" that de-watered the mines and the last one in use was replaced only two or three years ago. The china clay suspension may then run for several miles through pipes to the 'clay dries'. There most of the water is extracted and the china clay loaded into railway wagons, lorries or ships for export from Cornwall. The china clay is now a fine powder and for hundreds of feet around the clay dry the plants and trees become coated with a fine white dust. Waste water from the clay works passes into the streams, so that the land flows with 'milk' if not honey. This causes some silting and discolouration of the sea at the mouths of the streams.

Two-thirds of the annual production is exported overseas, to all parts of the world, mainly through the little ports of Charles-town, Par and Fowey. The china clay industry is still rapidly expanding and production is now about twice that of the peak pre-war years. It is also one of the main earners of foreign currency,

17

especially dollars. It has been estimated that the reserves are sufficient for the industry to go expanding till 3000 A.D.!

CORNISH FISHING

In the little ports and harbours all round the Cornish coast are still to be found the local fishing boats, and a brave sight they are when they put out in an evening to visit their crab and lobster pots or to spend the night fishing with the drift net or the "long line". Most of the fishermen in the little ports from Polperro to Porthleven and Port Isaac are inshore fishermen. The trawlers which stay out for a week or so at a time are mostly based on Newlyn which is also used by foreign boats as their temporary base. Newlyn is one of the most important fishing centres in Britain, and incidentally the place from which mean sea level is calculated.

Though the boats still make a brave show they are now only a small fraction of the numbers there were in the early years of the century. Ports which now have less than a dozen boats were then so full that it was almost possible to walk from deck to deck across the harbour. The number of men employed in fishing has also fallen, and worse, the average age of those remaining rises from year to year. The fisherman's earnings are entirely at the mercy of the elements and a job in which a man may earn £20 one week and then nothing for a month of stormy weather does not attract the young men.

The pilchards—which used to be one of the main catches— also seem to have deserted the trade. Some weeks the canners have hardly enough to keep the factories going and the fishermen make little because their catch is small. Then the boats will bring in a huge catch, more than the factories can manage, and most of the fishermen again make little because they are unable to sell their fish except for fertiliser.

The fishermen also complain of poaching, mainly by French and Breton boats, the depletion of breeding stocks by indiscriminate trawling, and the unfair competition from cheap South African tinned pilchards and Russian tinned crab. In addition to the Naval Fishery Protection Vessels the Cornwall Sea Fisheries Committee

18

MACKEREL BOATS COMING HOME
The late R. Morton Nance

also maintains its own launch to watch both for poachers and for shoals of fish.

Though the Cornish fishing industry has declined it is still one of the main sources of fish for Britain and a background to a whole way of life. It is a memorable experience to spend a night out in one of these little boats riding the Atlantic rollers or the Channel swells.

One ancient type of fishing which is still practised in Cornwall when the occasion arises is 'seining'. When a sizeable shoal appears near inshore boats are rowed around it, carrying a large net six feet deep which hangs vertically in the water. Under the directions of a "huer" on shore the boats drop this net around the shoal without disturbing it. The two ends are then brought together and the circumference gradually reduced until the sea within is a boiling mass of fish. This enclosure is towed as near the beach as possible and the fish are dipped out of it with other nets. Usually the whole village takes part in the labour, which may go on all day and night, and the proceeds are shared among all the helpers.

CORNISH FARMING

As Cornwall is well-known for its exports of milk, cream, eggs, flowers, early broccoli and potatoes it is not surprising that farming is one of its most important industries. But farming in Cornwall is very different from farming in England. By English standards most Cornish farms are small-holdings, and the fields themselves, especially in West Cornwall, are often minute compared to English fields. They are usually divided off not by wire fences or plain hedgerows but by 'Cornish hedges' which are massive dry stone walls, sometimes several feet thick and with an earthen core. Sometimes there is a hedgerow on top of this and occasionally even a footpath. These walls act as wind-breaks and the tiny fields of West Cornwall are sun-traps which enable the farmers to produce very early vegetables and flowers. Much Cornish farming is in fact market gardening.

Most of the farms are worked by the farmer and his family and few employ more than one or two labourers. Whereas in many

19

parts of rural England the farm workers tend to live in little villages, in much of rural Cornwall the purely agricultural village is the exception, and it is common for each farmstead and each cottage to be isolated from its neighbour. This difference has historical roots, for English farming grew from a communal system organised in manors while Cornish farming was more an individual and family concern.

ART IN CORNWALL

In Cornwall, before 1900, the production of great works of art was practically non-existent. There were fine craftsmen from very early times who worked the slate quarries of Delabole or who quarried and carved granite for many famous buildings, including St. Paul's, London, and indeed for the many fine bridges, churches, crosses, fonts, up and down the county. There were the very early artists who painted religious frescoes on the walls of churches like St. Breage and St. Just and the early wood-carvers who produced beautiful roodscreens or who carved bench-ends, but this was fine craftsmanship rather than a co-ordinated art movement. It was a popular folk art arising out of the needs of an isolated rural community.

Cornwall missed the great Celtic art movement of the seventh century, where Irish, Anglian and Continental influences mingled in a great flowering of British art. In Cornwall, there are no Lindisfarne Gospels and no Book of Kells. Indeed, there is no great Cornish figure in the artistic world, apart from Henry Bone, the enamellist, until John Opie (1761-1807). Opie, the youngest son of a mine carpenter, was born at St. Agnes in a small cob and thatched cottage. His artistic outlook was influenced by his surroundings, a highly productive mining area where, nevertheless, poverty and disputes between the mine-owners and the smelters were rife. Dr. Wolcot, a physician, amateur musician and artist, but best known for his satirical verses written under the name of Peter Pindar, taught Opie a great deal about technique and observation of character. He introduced him to his wide circle of friends, and for six years Opie painted portraits of many well-known Cornish families. Some fine groups of paintings exist from this early phase, notably those of the Prideaux of Padstow and of the Scobell family at Sancreed Vicarage.

20

- 35 -

THE HARBOUR AT ST. IVES

Claire White

Wolcot had a fine sense of the dramatic, and Opie owed his early fame in London to the Doctor's sponsorship of the 'wild boy' from Cornwall, 'an untaught genius', and also to the patronage of George III. For the first year, the forcefulness and vigour of his paintings made the fashionable world lionize him, but later his too blunt and honest attention to detail annoyed some o fhis sitters. However, Opie persevered and gradually became accepted into the world of art. Sir Joshua Reynolds became his friend and in 1787 he became an R.A. He painted many literary personalities at this time, but never completely forgot his Cornish background. "The Gentleman and the Miner" in the Royal Institution of Cornwall shows especially the rich variety and tones of colour which illuminated the West Cornwall mining landscape.

Since Opie's death there were few Cornish artists of distinction until the end of the last century. Then, with better transport and the continual urge of the artist to create new worlds, Cornwall was 'discovered'. The arists flocked first to Newlyn and then to St. Ives. The Newlyn School, which developed from 1880 onwards, grew up because of the dominant urge of the artist for the simple life—to paint life as it was, to escape from the pseudo-romantic paintings of the established art groups and to bring realism into painting. The group held that paintings should be done in 'plein-air' with local people and not artists' models. Many of their pictures are, in fact, still sentimental in background; but the figures of Newlyn fishermen, of the village school, of the narrow streets of Mousehole, or the Promenade at Penzance are nevertheless historical documents of the life of Cornwall in the early twentieth century.

Even today the artists and their studios are a notable feature of St. Ives and Newlyn and there is a small but growing number of native Cornish artists. One of them, Peter Lanyon was tragically killed in a gliding accident in 1964. Like painters of the early Newlyn School, he was very much a realist in that he painted what he saw, but there the comparison ends. Unlike most of the early Newlyn and St. Ives painters, he was himself Cornish and his work, like Opie's, evolved from the background in which he was born. Because of this, his paintings have the same vigour and sense of power which characterised Opie's best work. There is no sentimentalism here and in his 'abstract' paintings there is

21

a wholeness of vision which was not possible in earlier 'flat' paintings, Peter Lanyon not only painted the granitic moorland landscape, the rough rocks and seascape, the clear translucent air, which any visitor notices as different. He tried to put into his paintings the thoughts and feelings of those who are part of this land, of those who have gone before, or those who will be part of the Cornwall of the future. He has sensed the national consciousness of Cornwall. Like all great artists in different genres he has tried to 'see life steadily and see it whole'. While this may seem an impossibility, the fact that Peter Lanyon has tried to portray the hidden land of Cornwall and has been widely acclaimed in many parts of the world as a great artist, both of a region and as an influence on international modern art movements, suggests that he has succeeded where many other abstract artists have failed.

The work of Francis Cargeeg in copper is in complete contrast to the abstract art of Peter Lanyon, in that it is based on the traditional Celtic art forms of the greatest period of Celtic art. Here in copper, Francis Cargeeg moulds and re-creates patterns of Celtic knot-work, interlacing, and variations on the triskele. All his work is done by hand, and from flat sheets Cargeeg creates vases, mirrors, bowls of copper or great beauty and of high artistic merit. Francis Cargeeg is a Cornishman and though an individualist, as are all artists, his work is based on the copper found in the Cornish soil and the Celtic art forms found on many of the early Cornish crosses. From his vision of Celtic art he has created a new twentieth century Cornish art.

CORNISH WRITERS

As with Cornish artists, the consciousness of being Cornish has always been mirrored to a greater or lesser extent by Cornish writers. The founder of the modern Cornish movement in literature was Sir Arthur Quiller-Couch, (1863-1944), who, more than any other Cornish writer, established an especially Cornish, but at the same time nationally famous, literature. His novels of Cornwall, especially 'Troy Town', 'Sir John Constantine', 'The Splendid Spur', and 'Nick-Nan, Reservist', as well as many of his short stories made the mass of Cornish people aware for the first time of their heritage. He used many legends and local references to give his writings depth of background, but at the same time, like Thomas Hardy or the Lake Poets, his themes were universal and could be enjoyed

22

COPPER JAR BY FRANCIS CARGEEG
The late K. O. Chetwood-Aitken

by Cornish and non-Cornish alike.

One of "Q's" most interesting ventures was the publication under his editorship of the first "Cornish Magazine" in 1898 and 1899. Here he provided a training ground for many young writers who later became authorities on their own Cornish subjects:— R. Morton Nance, a later Grand Bard of the Cornish Gorsedd, who, with Henry Jenner and A. S. D. Smith, led the Cornish language movement and was one of its finest scholars; Charles Lee, whose "Cornish Tales", like those of "Q", have much of the essence of the Cornish character; Thurstan Peter whose "History of Cornwall for Schools" was produced in 1905, and which helped to stimulate the interest of young people in their native land.

Later magazines such as "Tre, Pol and Pen", "The West-Country Magazine", and, above all, "The Cornish Review", now all unfortunately defunct, provided scope for writers, artists and poets to express themselves about their native land. The present "Cornish Magazine", "New Cornwall", "An Lef Kernewek" (an all-Cornish quarterly), and "Old Cornwall", all in their different ways, try to keep interest in Cornwall and Cornish consciousness vividly alive.

There are also, certain modern writers who should be mentioned. Foremost among them, A. L. Rowse, the historian, who, like "Q", has brought all the wealth of his scholarship to bear on a Cornish subject in his book "Tudor Cornwall", and his sensitivity to the Cornish scene in his books of poems. There are, too, writers like Rosalie Glyn Grylls, Anne Treneer and Lady Vyvyan, and, of course, many others who have studied perceptively the Cornwall they have known and loved. And finally, there is Jack Clemo, the poet of the china-clay land, who has made the white moon-cratered landscape round St. Austell his own particular poetic inspiration. With Charles Causley, he is very much a poet of the Cornwall of today.

CORNISH SPORTS

Hurling, like the Padstow 'Obby 'Oss and the Helston Hal an Tow, has a long tradition behind it. Indeed, there is a suggestion

23

that the battle between two teams for the possession of the silver ball originally represented the battle between winter and summer, while the throwing up of the silver ball symbolised the ascendency of the sun in the heavens. Certainly, hurling has long been a popular sport which has survived unaltered up to the present day in Cornwall, but which was formerly played in other parts of Britain, especially Wales and Scotland, and also in Brittany where it was known as 'la soule'.

In Cornwall, hurling takes place in St. Ives on Feast Monday, but it is to St. Columb Major on Shrove Tuesday and on the Saturday of the following week, that the visitor should go to see the game in all its glory. Here the two teams represent Town and Country and the aim of each team is to take the ball to its own goal at the other end of the parish. Formerly, this was a bloodthirsty sport, men fighting and wrestling with those who had the lucky ball, but today, though shops and offices are all shuttered and barricaded, little damage but bruises and cuts result. The St. Columb ball is inscribed:—

Town and country do your best
For in this parish I must rest.

but many of the older hurling balls were inscribed with the Cornish motto "Gwary whek yu gwary tek" (Fair play is good play) which illustrates the spirit of fierce but friendly rivalry which is now the key-note of the game.

Skill in tackling opponents in the game of hurling was due mainly ,to another typical Cornish sport which still flourishes, though in a restricted form; that is Cornish wrestling. This, like hurling, was once popular all over Britain and in Brittany, and in the mass emigration of Cornishmen in the nineteenth century the sport was taken to all parts of the world. Now alas, it is not so widely followed as it used to be, but the formation of the Cornish Wrestling Association in 1923 has done much to halt the effects of tournaments every year and also some small contests and exhibicommercially organised sports and mass media such as television. For many years the Association organised annual wrestling tournaments between Bretons and Cornishmen and local tournaments throughout Cornwall. Now, there are four or five big

24

EVENING AT TINTAGEL
The late K. O. Chetwood-Aitken

tions at local fairs and feasts. At one school, Truro Cathedral School, the boys can learn Cornish wrestling and so there is at least a youthful contingent of Cornish wrestlers.

The modern equivalent of both hurling and wrestling is Cornish rugby. While the rules are the same as those of rugby football all over the world, the enthusiasm, vigour and rivalry with which the game is played are unequalled except perhaps in Wales, that other great Rugby country. Go to a local Derby, especially Camborne v. Redruth, and hear the famous Redruth roar and the loud and uninhibited vocal participation of the great crowds watching. One can imagine these men as part of the 20,000 Cornishmen who threatened to rescue Bishop Trelawney, or that vast army in the 1497 Rebellion that terrified the countryside as it marched purpose-fully to battle beneath the walls of London.

CORNISH SPECIALITIES

Traditional foods have lost some of their importance since the production of tinned and frozen foods, the use of refrigeration and better transport facilities. This is true of the whole of the country. However, in Cornwall as in many rural areas, traditional foods do survive, and are welcomed as an antidote to the standardisation of food which is taking place all over the world. The most famous Cornish food is the 'pasty' which can contain almost anything from jam to leeks or egg and bacon, but which usually has beef, onion, turnip and sliced potato in its pastry case. There is also saffron cake, a great delicacy especially when home-baked, and home-made splits topped with jam and Cornish clotted cream cannot be equalled. Look out especially for some of the less well-known foods, heavy cake, or home-made potato cakes, still a great favourite with Cornish people. There are also marinated pilchards, and 'scrawled' (or grilled) mackerel, as well as 'fairings' or biscuits originally made and sold at local fairs. Home-made drinks are still to be found, 'herby' or nettle beer, sloe gin, elderberry or blackberry wine being the favourites. To sample many of these fine traditional foods, one should stay with a Cornish farmer's wife, as many of them are not on sale commercially, and unfortunately, of those which are, a high standard of quality does not *always* apply.

25

CORNWALL TODAY AND IN THE FUTURE

Even today Cornwall retains, both superficially and hidden in the depths of her being, the marks of her distinct and separate origin. Cornwall is not just another English county but a Celtic country in its own right. Its people retain, often sub-consciously, their sense of nationality, their own attitude to life, and the foundations of their native culture.

Economically, two of Cornwall's traditional industries, mining and fishing, have declined to a low level, but, given suitable conditions, may yet revive in the future. China clay working, agriculture and tourism are fairly flourishing but Cornwall's economy is not sufficiently diversified. A slump in any one of the three major industries could cause immeasurable hardship. Even now the ratio of unemployment is higher than the national average. The County Council is making strenuous efforts to attract new light industries, and has had some success. Many people are striving for better economic, social and cultural conditions in Cornwall, but the rock on which all efforts seem to founder is the ignorance of local conditions shown by the authorities in Bristol and London. The most forcible opinions about this are expressed by MEBYON KERNOW (The Sons of Cornwall) which exists to further the interests of Cornwall.

Mebyon Kernow believes that Cornwall needs a stable and broad-based economy and a developing cultural life, forward-looking but based on traditional Cornish ways and not solely on an Anglo-American mass culture. In general, its members advocate for mining and other extractive industries a realistic system of tax relief like those in Ireland and Canada. This would encourage renewed development in these industries. Mebyon Kernow has long advocated the extension of fishing limits and does not feel that the recent extensions made by the British Government are in themselves sufficient. An alternative proposal is that there should be an inner zone of six miles from a cape-to-cape base-line reserved for local inshore fishermen — drifting and crabbing — and an outer zone of a further six miles forbidden to foreign trawlers with the authority of the Local Sea Fisheries Committee extended to at least the inner

26

- 44 -

six miles instead of being restricted to the three mile territorial waters. Mebyon Kernow wishes to see the maintenance the Cornish railway system and its co-ordination with other forms of transport under a Cornish Transport Committee so that the community and its industries can be properly served. Even greater efforts to establish new light industries are advocated. The tourist trade and agriculture must take their proper place in Cornish economy, and rural amenities, such as mains water, drainage and electricity, local transport and social centres, must be improved to reduce the drift from the land as well as the drift from Cornwall. In this connection it is a matter of principle that for posts in Cornwall the Cornishman, if equally qualified, should have preference over candidates from outside.

On the cultural side, Mebyon Kernow advocates the establishment of a University in Cornwall and, greater emphasis in education on Cornwall and its own culture. Mebyon Kernow supports wholeheartedly other Cornish societies in their efforts to encourage the use of Cornish, to maintain traditional Cornish culture, and to present the true facts of the history of the Cornish nation. Equally it supports the strengthening of the links between Cornwall and the other Celtic countries.

Mebyon Kernow sees little prospect of achieving the reforms it desires while Cornwall is neglected and its interests over-ruled by Whitehall bureaucrats, and therefore believes that the future of Cornwall can only be ensured by control of Cornish affairs by Cornish people. Cornwall, after all, is slightly larger than Luxembourg—a full member of the European Common Market— and Cornish people are no less intelligent than Maltese or Jamaicans and so are equally capable of running their own affairs. This would be a form of self-government within Great Britain—a system that already works well in the Isle of Man, the Channel Isles and Northern Ireland.

The emergence over the last fifteen years of a thoughtful, vocal and consciously Cornish group is one of the most promising signs that Cornwall will continue to exist as a Celtic country and not decline into merely an administrative division of England.

27

SOME BOOKS FOR FURTHER READING

Baker, Denys Val—The Cornish Review, 1949-51.
Cornwall's Art Colony by the Sea, 1959.
The Minack Theatre, 1960.
Berry, Claude—Cornwall (The County Books Series), 1949.
Portrait of Cornwall, 1963
Clemo, Jack—Map of Clay, and Other Poems, 1961.
Coate, Mary—Cornwall in the Great Civil War, 1933.
Doble, G. H.—Lives of the Cornish Saints (issued in pamphlets), reprinted and re-edited by D. Attwater in bound volumes, 1960 onwards.
Elliott-Binns, L. E.—Medieval Cornwall, 1955.
Grylls, Rosalie Glyn—Trelawny, 1950.
GWRYANS AN BYS (Cornish Miracle Play with English translation), reprinted by Federation of Old Cornwall Societies.
Halliday, F. E.—The Legend of the Rood, 1955.
A History of Cornwall, 1959.
Hawkey, Muriel (ed)—A Cornish Chorus, 1948.
Henderson, C.—Essays in Cornish History, 1935.
(reprinted 1963)
Hooper, E. G. R.—Revised Edition of R. Morton Nance and A. S. D. Smith's translation of St. Mark's Gospel.
An Awayl herwyth Sen Mark, 1960.
Revised Edition of A. S. D. Smith's Lessons in Spoken Cornish, 1962.
& White, G. P. (ed) Lyver Hymnys ha Salmow, 1963.
Cornish Hymn Book with some Psalms.
Jenkin, A. K. Hamilton—The Story of Cornwall, 1934.
reprinted as paper-back, 1962.
Cornwall and Its People, 1945.
The Cornish Miner, 1927.
Jenner, Henry—Handbook of the Cornish Language, 1904.
Martin, Edith (ed)—Cornish Recipes, Ancient and Modern.
Nance, R. Morton—Cornish For All, 1929, revised 1949.
A Guide to Cornish Place-names, 1951.
English-Cornish Dictionary, 1952.
Cornish-English Dictionary, revised 1955.
& Smith A. S. D.—Extracts from Cornish Texts, with English translation, Nos I-VI.

23

Nankivell, Florence (ed)—Principal Antiquities of the Newquay-
Padstow District, 1962.
Pelmear, Kenneth—Rugby in the Duchy, 1960.
Pevsner, N.—The Buildings of England:— Cornwall, 1951.
Pollard, Peggy—Cornwall, 1947.
Pool, P. A. S.—Cornish for Beginners, 1962.
"Q"—Novels published by Dent & Son Ltd.
"Q" Anthology, edited F. Brittain, 1948.
Rowe, John—Cornwall in the Industrial Revolution, 1953.
Rowse, A. L.—Tudor Cornwall, 1941.
Poems of a Decade, 1941.
Poems Chiefly Cornish, 1943.
Poems of Deliverance, 1946.
West-Country Stories, 1945.
(ed) The West in English History, 1949.
Smith, A. S. D.—(Caradar) Cornish Simplified, 1939.
The Story of the Cornish Language, its Extinction and Revival,
1947.
Trystan hag Ysolt (Memorial Volume), 1951.
Thomas, A. C.—Gwithian, Ten Years' Work, 1958.
& Pool, P. A. S.—Guide to the Principal Antiquities of the
Land's End District, 1957.
Treneer, Anne—Cornish Years, 1949.
School House in the Wind, 1944.
Happy Button (Short Stories), 1950.
The Mercurial Chemist (Sir Humphrey Davy) 1963
Vyvyan, C. C.—Our Cornwall, 1948.

MAGAZINES

AN LEF KERNEWEK—editor E. G. R. Hooper, 16 Trevu Road,
Camborne (quarterly, in Cornish, duplicated).
CORNISH ARCHAEOLOGY—editor A. C. Thomas, journal of
the Cornwall Archaeological Society (sec. Mrs. Nankivell,
"Bosgea", Steeple Lane, St. Ives).
CORNISH MAGAZINE—editor J. Saxton, Penpol Press,
Falmouth (monthly magazine of general Cornish interest).
JOURNAL OF THE ROYAL INSTITUTION OF CORNWALL,
County Museum, River Street, Truro.
NEW CORNWALL—editors, Richard and Ann Jenkin, An
Gernyk, Leedstown, Hayle (six issues a year, duplicated).
OLD CORNWALL—journal of the Fed. of Old Cornwall Societies
(sec. Mr. L. R. Moir, "Pengarth", Carbis Bay, St. Ives).

A Cornish Timeline 1965-2005.

(selections)

There is no space to look back in detail at previous events and initiatives, but I should mention the death of Robert Morton Nance second Grand Bard in 1959, the opening of the Tamar Road Bridge in 1961,which opened up Cornwall to more and more tourists, and the ground-breaking first Cornish Language wedding in recent times on 3rd. October 1964 of Susan Chapman and Malcolm Smith. Cornish flags and a Cornish-speaking clergyman were in short supply! Goonhilly Earth Satellite Station opened and linked Cornwall and the world in 1962.

1965 – *Cornwall the Hidden Land* published.

1966 – Death of Harold Hayman, Cornish-born and much-respected Labour MP from 1955 onwards, one of Cornwall's very few Labour MPs. *Canow Kernow* published, with 9 songs in the Cornish language, collected by Inglis Gundry.

1967 – Colin Murley won the first ever MK County Council seat at St. Day & Lanner.

1969 – Int.Celtic Congress, Kenegie, Gulval. Professor Charles Thomas, President. The Ordinalia acted in English by Bristol University students at Perran Round.

1970 – RGJ first Mebyon Kernow parliamentary candidate. Lodenek Press set up by Donald Rawe of Padstow. Leonard Truran organised sales of Cornish stamps and Cornish calendars. He later set up a publishing business *Dyllansow Truran.*

1973 – In April the Institute of Cornish Studies opened at Pool, Redruth, managed jointly by Cornwall County Council and Exeter University. Professor Charles Thomas, the new Director, gave the inaugural address. His lecture was on *The Importance of Being Cornish in Cornwall.* RGJ new Chairman of MK. *Crowdy Crawn* published, the first record in modern times including songs in Cornish, written by Dick

Gendall & sung by Brenda Wootton.(Sentinel records). Gwryans an Bys produced by Donald Rawe/Kernow Productions at Perran Round.

1975 – Formation of the Cornish Nationalist Party by James Whetter.

1976 – RGJ Grand Bard of Gorseth Kernow (1976-1983).

1978 – Fifty years since the formation of Gorseth Kernow.

1979 – RGJ contested Euro-Parlt. Seat on a 'Cornwall Seat' platform. Had 10,000 votes. First Celtic Festival, *Lowender Peran,* held in Perranporth. *Canow an Weryn Hedhyu* published by Lodenek Press. (24 songs, 22 in Cornish)

1981 – In December, the Penlee Lifeboat was lost with all hands off Lamorna.

1982 – Colin Lawry elected on to Penwith District Council. International Celtic Congress, Ponsandane, Penzance, with emphasis on Celtic youth. Radio Cornwall started, the first purpose-built local radio station. Cornwall Heritage Trust formed, to protect & conserve Cornwall's buildings and natural heritage.

1983 – 1st. Eisteddfod of Cornwall/Esethvos Kernow set up by Gorseth Kernow, to widen an appreciation of Cornish cultural, linguistic and historical life. First novel in Cornish published by Melville Bennetto, *An Gurun Wosek a Geltya*/The Bloody Crown of Celtya.

1984 – Cornwall Innovation Centre established. *An Canker Seth* produced by John King for ITV, a series of programmes teaching Cornish through film. The first.

1985 – Colin Lawry elected to CCC. 2nd. term of RGJ as Grand Bard (1985-1988). Only R.M. Nance served longer. CCC agreed to fly the Cornish flag outside County Hall. The price of tin slumped, which caused the slow death of Cornish mining.

1986 – Geevor Tin Mine closed. A Cornish March through the streets of London did not save it. David Penhaligon popular Liberal MP for Truro, killed in a car crash. Known as "The Voice of Cornwall".

1987 – Britain's First Air Ambulance launched in Cornwall. Funded by local public subscription.

1988 – International Celtic Congress at Newquay. Theme *Cornwall & the Sea*. CoSERG (Cornwall Social & Economic Research Group) produced a critique of official socio-economic policies entitled *Cornwall at the Crossroads*. RGJ began *Delyow Derow/Oak Leaves,* a literary magazine in the Cornish language.

1990 – Cornish Association of S. Australia, celebrated their centenary with a banquet. Loveday Jenkin, 2nd daughter of RGJ and ATJ elected as MK Party chairman.

1991 - Britain's first commercial Wind Farm opened at Delabole. A new anemone the *St. Piran Anemone,* bred at Duchy College. The *Made in Cornwall,* Cornwall County Council Approved Origin Scheme started, *to promote and protect the identity of Cornish made products.* Cornwall Rugby Team beat Yorkshire at Twickenham. 40,000 attend from *Trelawny's Army!* First win since 1908.

1993 – Bi-centenary of Royal Cornwall Show. June 23rd. Tate St.Ives opened to the public. The Lost Gardens of Heligan re-opened by Tim Smit. Philip Knight and Forbidden Fruit first to win for Cornwall the Pan-Celtic Song Contest in Killarney, Eire.

1994 – ATJ elected as first woman Deputy Grand Bard of Gorseth Kernow. Death of Jack Clemo, Cornish poet of the Clay Country. The Trevithick Trust set up. Loveday Jenkin stood for the European Parliamentary seat. *CornishWorld/Bys Kernowyon,* started by Philip Hosken – a ground-breaking achievement.

1995 – Loveday Jenkin elected as MK councillor on Crowan Parish Council and Kerrier District Council.

1997 – Dick Cole became party chairman of MK, a position he still holds. RGJ became Life President. First International Celtic Film and Television Festival held at St. Ives. *Keskerdh Kernow/Cornwall Marches On* provided a great impetus for Cornish aspirations and identity, with thousands marching to London from Cornwall to commemorate the original March by An Gof and Flamank in 1497. The signing of the *Blackheath Declaration.* ATJ became the first ever woman Grand Bard at the Bodmin Gorsedd. Death of A.L. Rowse, Cornish writer and historian, and Helena Saunders nee Charles, founder of Mebyon Kernow. Andrew George was elected to Parliament for the Liberal Democrats, in May and spoke in Cornish in his adoption speech in the House of Commons on 22 May.

1998 - The death of mining in Cornwall with the closure of South Crofty, the last working mine. Cornish Solidarity is born. *…but when the fish and tin are gone, what are our Cornish lads to do…*(Roger Bryant). Cornwall recognised in the NUTS 2 document as a separate economic region from Devon, with its own culture and identity. This opened the doors to Objective 1 Funding for poor areas of Europe. Cornwall County Council named several mining areas in Cornwall as a potential Cornish Mining World Heritage Site. The search started for world- wide recognition. The first Holyer an Gof Award for publishers set up in memory of Leonard Truran, by Gorseth Kernow. St. Piran Trust set up

1999 – Cornwall won the County Rugby Championship at Twickenham, defeating Gloucestershire. *Last one to leave Cornwall, put out the light!* Dick Cole (MK), elected to Restormel District Council. 450th anniversary of the 1549 Prayerbook Rebellion commemorated with a march from Cornwall to Exeter, and the planting of 450 black and white Cornish flags outside the cathedral. Total eclipse darkens Cornwall. Cornwall is awarded Objective 1 status as one of the poorest and most deprived areas in Britain. *Breaking the Chains* published by John Angarrack, dealing with *propaganda, censorship, deception and the manipulation of public opinion in Cornwall.* It challenged many accepted myths about Cornwall. Pete Berryman and West won with An

Arvor at the Pan-Celtic Festival in Eire. A tripartite Gorsedd (Wales, Cornwall & Brittany) held in Brittany to commemorate 100 years of the Breton Gorsedd.

2000 – International Celtic Congress held in Bude in April. 85,000 Millennium books published for all Cornish school children, *Kernow bys Vyken/Cornwall for Ever.* It was launched by Prince Charles, who spoke of Cornwall as a country! It helped to awaken the consciousness of Cornish school children to their special heritage. The Declaration for a Cornish Assembly was signed by over 50,000 people, a tenth of the Cornish population. It was an MK initiative, launched on St. Piran's Day. This led to the founding of the broad-based Cornish Constitutional Convention by Bert Biscoe, Andrew George, Dick Cole and others in July. The government was uninterested, and is still unsupportive, though the Liberal Democrats paid lip-service to the idea. No concerted action yet! The first part of the Ordinalia, *Origo Mundi/The Origin of the World* spectacularly produced as a community play in English but with some Cornish by Dominic Knutton at St. Just. Another first after four centuries. In July, there was a March and the unveiling of a Memorial Stone by ATJ to those who died in the 1549 Prayerbook Rebellion at Fenny Bridges in Devon, the site of a major massacre. In August, a similar stone was unveiled by ATJ in Penryn, to commemorate the part Penryn played in the Prayerbook Rebellion and in the preservation of the Cornish language at Glasney.

2001 – The Eden Project opened in March near St.Austell. The second International Celtic Film and Television Festival held in Truro. The second part of the Ordinalia, *Passio Christi/ The Passion of Christ* performed at St. Just. A replica of the first successful Trevithick steam engine went up Camborne Hill on Christmas Eve. Conan Jenkin, 2nd son of RGJ and ATJ stood for a parliamentary seat for MK.

2002 – Tony Blair said the following in a *Times* article on 12 February: *It is intrinsic in the nature of the Union (UK) that we have multiple political allegiances; we can comfortably be Scottish and British or Cornish and British or Geordie and British or Pakistani and British...*

The first Dehwelans, a Homecoming of Cornish Exiles from around the world, chaired by ATJ, was held at Pendennis Castle, Falmouth in May. *Testament Noweth* by Nicholas Williams of Trinity College, Dublin, first published. The Ordinalia, part three, *Resurrexio Domini/The Resurrection of our Lord* produced at St. Just. Cornwall recognised on the European Charter for Minority Languages, after a six year struggle. Death of Richard Jenkin - A funeral service wholly in Cornish. John Angarrack published his second book, *Our Future is History - A Study of Identity, Law and The Cornish Question.*

2003 – National Maritime Museum, Cornwall, opened to the public in March. A new Cornish literary magazine *Scryfa* appeared, edited by Simon Parker. Strategy Advisory Group set up to study how to proceed in the implementation of the Charter for Cornish, under Jory Ansell and with Jenefer Lowe as facilitator. Rachel and Common Ground won at the Pan-Celtic with *Tir Kemmyn.* 50 years since the formation of Bude Surf Lifesaving Club, the first in Britain. First production of *A Sense of Place* for the general public. Children learn about their own history, language and culture under the direction of Will Coleman. Charles Causley died, one of Cornwall's greatest poets.

2004 - The second Dewhelans, the Homecoming of Cornish exiles, was held at Barrowfields, Newquay. *Hellfire Corner,* a play about Cornish Rugby, written by D.M.Thomas, performed at the Hall for Cornwall. First extended Holyer an Gof Awards (5) for Cornish publishers in memory of Leonard Truran, held at Ottakars, Truro and sponsored by them and the Eden Project. Organised by ATJ. Publication of *Henry and Katharine Jenner, a Celebration of Cornwall's Culture, Language and Identity,* edited by Derek Williams. Publication of *The New Testament in Cornish* by Keith Syed. A service in Truro Cathedral to present the Archbishop of Canterbury with a copy. Languages used - English, Welsh, Cornish and Latin. The Tremough Campus opened at Penryn, as part of the University of Exeter in Cornwall. The Camborne School of Mines and the Institute of Cornish Studies moved to the campus. Loveday Jenkin became the first Cabinet Member of MK on Kerrier District Council. *Keltyon Bew* won at the Pan-Celtic with *Transporthys.*

A combined and shortened version of the 3 Ordinalia plays performed at St. Just.

2005 – Early death of Nick Darke, nationally known Cornish playwright. Holyer an Gof Publishers' Awards further extended, with 8 awards, two to authors/publishers from overseas. In September the first major conference on *The Future of Cornish* was held at the University at Penryn, to implement the Cornish Strategy on the language. Attended by 120 and with speakers from Wales, Isle of Man and Scotland as well as Cornwall. An excavation of St. Piran's second church started at Perranporth. The September edition of *Cornish World/Bys Kernowyon* published an important article, *Cornwall not England. What makes the Duchy unique?* 1st. Poetry Cornwall Festival at Chacewater, organised by Les Merton. In December, *Cornwall the Hidden Land, published with* additions, including a forty year Cornish Timeline 1965-2005, of important Cornish events. *Skywardya* led by Matthew Clark, won at the Pan-Celtic Festival in Ireland.

Postscript

While a timeline throws up questions and some answers about Cornwall and shows a gradual progression in many areas over the last forty years, it does not clearly emphasise the continuing poverty of the region. Unemployment has been very high, and this year, the Bishop of Truro launched a *Poverty is History* campaign. Second home-owners have bought up picturesque dwellings all over Cornwall and the young cannot find anywhere to live. This has meant a continual drain of our young people out of Cornwall. The cost of houses has risen faster than any other area of Britain. There are too many cars on our roads, and not enough public rural transport. There are not enough measures to care for our special natural and built environment. The government continues to neglect rural areas, and the Cornish are becoming a minority in their own land.

However, there have been some successes too. More inward investment through Objective 1, including for the new university, though it should have a more Cornish dimension; more innovative industry, particularly through the Cornish food markets, publishing and other small scale enterprises; the visit of cruise ships to the Port of Falmouth, an important maritime development; other financial successes like Eden; a huge flowering of cultural and artistic talents through Kneehigh and other groups, and the new Arts Marketing initiative. The Cornish language is becoming more respected and more widely used. There is a much more positive attitude in Cornwall with more people, more often, standing up for a Cornish dimension to our lives. Cornwall is no longer "The Hidden Land," nor are its people invisible! The battle is not won, but the fight for recognition continues. *Kernow bys Vyken.*

Ann Trevenen Jenkin © Leedstown, Kernow. October 2005.

(*Abbreviations: RGJ* = Richard Garfield Jenkin. *ATJ* = Ann Trevenen Jenkin)

Publications by Richard and Ann Jenkin
(New Cornwall Publications & Noonvares Press)

Crygyon Kernow Ogas ha Pell -Cornish Ripples Near and Far by Ann Trevenen Jenkin. Published 2005 by Noonvares Press. A second poetry book. Cost £7.00. ISBN 09524601 6 5.
Cornwall the Hidden Land by Richard & Ann Jenkin. Facsimile re-print 2005 by Noonvares Press with an additional introduction by Professor Philip Payton, and a new Cornish time-line 1965-2005 by Ann Trevenen Jenkin. ISBN:09524601 5 7. Cost £5.00.
An Ky a Gerdhas bys dhe Loundres translated from the English by Vanessa Beeman. Published by Noonvares Press 2004 at £7.50. ISBN 0 9524601 4 9. Holyer an Gof Commendation 2005.
The Dog who Walked to London by Ann Trevenen Jenkin. Published in 2003 by Noonvares Press. ISBN 09524601 3 0. Holyer an Gof Commendation July 2004.
Leedstown Millennium Diary edited by Ann Trevenen Jenkin with Leedstown WI members. Not published. Original in Cornwall Record Office, Truro. 2000.